# POCKET PETS

ALVIN SILVERSTEIN · VIRGINIA SILVERSTEIN · LAURA SILVERSTEIN NUNN

TWENTY-FIRST CENTURY BOOKS
BROOKFIELD, CONNECTICUT

Cover photograph courtesy of Animals Animals (© Charles Palek)

Photographs courtesy of Animals Animals: pp. 6 (© Robert Maier), 10 (© Michael Dick),
14 (© Robert Maier), 18 (© Zig Leszczynski), 22 (© Zig Leszczynski), 26 (© John A.L. Cooke),
30 (© Gerard Lacz), 38 (© Robert Maier), 42 (© Robert Maier); The National Audubon
Society Collection/Photo Researchers: p. 34 (© Nick Bergkessel)

Cover Design by Karen Quigley
Interior Design by Claire Fontaine

Library of Congress Cataloging-in-Publication Data

Silverstein, Alvin.
Pocket Pets/Alvin Silverstein, Virginia Silverstein, Laura Silverstein Nunn.
p. cm. — (What a pet!)
Includes bibliographical references (p.      ) and Index.
Summary: Discusses the pros and cons of keeping various small pets such as chinchillas, hamsters,
gerbils, and mice, examining their care, feeding, and emotional needs.
ISBN 0-7613-1370-2 (lib. bdg.)
1. Pets—Juvenile literature. [1. Pets.] I. Silverstein, Virginia. II. Nunn, Laura Silverstein. III. Title. IV.
Series: Silverstein, Alvin. What a pet!

SF416.2.S56  2000
636.088'7—dc21                                                                                              98-47616
                                                                                                                  CIP
                                                                                                                   AC

Published by Twenty-First Century Books
A Division of The Millbrook Press, Inc.
2 Old New Milford Road
Brookfield, CT 06804

Visit us at our Web site: www.millbrookpress.com

# CONTENTS

CHINCHILLA . . . . . . . . . . . . . . . . . . . . . 6

DEGU . . . . . . . . . . . . . . . . . . . . . . . . . 10

HAMSTER . . . . . . . . . . . . . . . . . . . . . . 14

GERBIL . . . . . . . . . . . . . . . . . . . . . . . . 18

DUPRASI . . . . . . . . . . . . . . . . . . . . . . . 22

RAT . . . . . . . . . . . . . . . . . . . . . . . . . . 26

MOUSE . . . . . . . . . . . . . . . . . . . . . . . . 30

FLYING SQUIRREL . . . . . . . . . . . . . . . . 34

GUINEA PIG . . . . . . . . . . . . . . . . . . . . 38

RABBIT . . . . . . . . . . . . . . . . . . . . . . . . 42

NOT A PET! . . . . . . . . . . . . . . . . . . . . 46

FOR FURTHER INFORMATION . . . . . . . . . . 47

INDEX . . . . . . . . . . . . . . . . . . . . . . . . 48

# WHAT A PET!

**THIS SERIES WILL GIVE** you information about some well-known animals and some unusual ones. It will help you to select a pet suitable for your family and for where you live. It will also tell you about animals that should *not* be pets. It is important for you to understand that many people who work with animals are strongly opposed to keeping *any* wild creature as a pet.

People tend to want to keep exotic animals. But they forget that often it is illegal to have them as pets, or that they require a great deal of special care and will never really become good pets. A current fad of owning an exotic animal may quickly pass, and the animals suffer. Their owners may abandon them in an effort to return them to the wild, even though the animals can no longer survive there. Or they may languish in small cages without proper food and exercise.

*Before* selecting any animal as a pet, it is a good idea to learn as much as you can about it. This series will help you, and your local veterinarian and the ASPCA are good sources of information. You should also find out if it is endangered. Phone numbers for each state wildlife agency can be found on the Internet at

**http://www.animalsforsale.com/states.htm**

and you can get an updated list of endangered and threatened species on the Internet at

**http://jjwww.fws.gov/r9endspp/endspp.html** "Endangered Species Home Page, U.S. Fish & Wildlife Service"

Any pet is a big responsibility—*your* responsibility. The most important thing to keep in mind when selecting a pet is the welfare of the animal.

5

## FAST FACTS

| | |
|---|---|
| Scientific name | *Chinchilla lanigera* in Family Chinchillidae, Order Rodentia |
| Cost | May range from $50 to $100 |
| Food | Chinchilla pellets, hay, lawn trimmings, raw vegetables, corn, apples, sunflower seeds, carrots, twigs |
| Housing | A wire mesh cage should include a tree branch for climbing, a sleeping box, a water bottle, a dust box for bathing, and a wood block for gnawing. |
| Training | Be very gentle and use treats, such as raisins, to train. |
| Special notes | A special permit may be required to keep chinchillas. |

# CHINCHILLA

COULD YOU FIT A CHINCHILLA in your pocket? Probably not. But these soft, adorable critters are often called pocket pets. This term originally described small rodents that are kept as pets and could fit into your pocket, like hamsters and gerbils. But these days, "pocket pets" also includes a variety of other not-so-small rodents and other animals.

Chinchillas are exotic animals. That's what makes them so interesting but a bit more expensive than other pocket pets. They are also a lot of fun to watch and much less trouble to care for than other exotic animals. For these reasons, chinchillas are becoming increasingly popular as pets.

## The Need for Gnawing

*Chinchillas are rodents. This is a very large and varied group of mammals (probably more than half of all the mammal species) that includes mostly small animals. Rats, mice, hamsters, gerbils, guinea pigs, squirrels, chipmunks, beavers, gophers, and porcupines are all rodents.*

*All rodents have one main thing in common—their teeth. A rodent's four long front teeth (incisors) keep growing throughout its entire life. The word* rodent *comes from the Latin* rodere, *which means "to gnaw." Rodents need to gnaw on things constantly to keep the incisors worn down. If a rodent is unable to wear its teeth down for some reason, the teeth will continue to grow so long that it will be unable to close its mouth and may die.*

*You may find your chinchilla pet gnawing on things in the middle of the night. Like most other rodents, chinchillas are nocturnal; they are active at night and sleep during the day. Some rodent pets, however, can change their schedule to suit yours.*

# ON THE BRINK OF EXTINCTION

Chinchillas have been popular for hundreds of years, but not as pets. Instead, they were valued for their pelts—their soft, thick fur. Spanish explorers conquered the chinchilla's native lands in South America in the 1500s and took pelts back with them when they returned to Europe. Soon chinchilla fur became well known in Europe and was used to trim royal robes and gowns. Only the wealthy could afford to pay the high prices for the fur.

Chinchillas were in great demand, especially in the 1700s and 1800s. It takes more than a hundred skins to make a chinchilla coat, and hundreds of thousands of chinchillas were trapped and killed each year. By the early 1900s, these rodents had been hunted so much that they were almost extinct in their native Peru, Bolivia, and Chile. Finally, the governments of these countries made it illegal to trap and kill chinchillas.

# CAPTIVE BREEDING

Over the years, many attempts were made to bring chinchillas down from the mountains to breed in captivity. Many failed. But in 1918, Mathias F. Chapman, a mining engineer from California who was working in Chile, became interested in chinchillas when he bought one from a local Chilean native to keep as a pet. Chapman worked out a careful plan for gradually getting the animals used to lower altitudes and finally got approval from the reluctant Chilean government to capture and transport chinchillas to the United States, to raise for the fur market.

By 1923, Chapman and his crew had brought eleven chinchillas down from the Andes. When they arrived in San Pedro, California, there were twelve—a baby had been born! Chapman set up the first successful breeding facility in California. Today, there are thousands of chinchilla breeding farms across the country. Nearly all of today's chinchillas come from Chapman's original stock. (The few remaining in the wild are on the Endangered Species List.) Although most are still raised for their pelts, more and more chinchillas are being sold as pets.

## Only Semidomesticated

*Chinchillas are not domesticated animals. Although they have been bred in captivity since the early 1900s, no attempts have been made to select animals to produce desirable traits. For instance, calm chinchillas that are bred with other calm chinchillas produce offspring that can live contentedly with humans. Problem animals would not be used in selective breeding. However, since chinchillas are not selectively bred at present, they are considered wild animals used for commercial purposes, but not quite domesticated.*

# CHINCHILLAS AS PETS

The chinchilla looks a little like a rabbit, has a bushy tail like a squirrel, and hops like a kangaroo on its large hind feet with rubberlike soles. Chinchillas are usually blue-gray, although they may also be beige, cream, black, or white. They may grow 10 to 14 inches (25 to 36 centimeters) long, with a 6- to 8-inch (15- to 20-centimeter) tail, and weigh only 1 to 2 pounds (0.5 to 1 kilogram).

Chinchillas are delicate yet hardy animals. Their native habitat is the snow-covered Andes Mountains of South America, where they live in rocky burrows at altitudes above 8,000 feet (2,440 meters). In the wild, they have adapted to very harsh conditions—a lack of water, dry air and land, and bitter cold temperatures. The chinchillas' warm, thick fur helps them to survive the often frigid temperatures. For this reason, chinchillas cannot handle temperatures warmer than 80°F (about 27°C) and should be protected from the heat.

Chinchillas are social animals. In their home in the wild, they lived in large colonies. Pet chinchillas can live alone or in pairs. (Some are more sociable than others.) Housing two males together, however, will result in fighting.

Chinchillas are often shy and frightened around people, though they are not aggressive by nature. The more often a chinchilla is handled, the friendlier it will become. The younger the chinchilla, the easier it will be to tame. After a while, it may rest comfortably in your hands or even sit on your shoulder. Some chinchillas can be trained to do little tricks, like sitting up to "beg" or coming when their name is called.

Unlike most other animals, chinchillas do not have any odor. They are very clean and need to take a dust bath at least once or twice a week to get rid of any extra oils and dirt in the coat. (Use a shallow pan filled with special chinchilla dust sold in some pet stores.) Never give a chinchilla a water bath. The water will ruin its coat, removing the natural oils and its ability to keep warm.

When cared for properly, a chinchilla pet can be a longtime companion. Chinchillas live longer than any other rodent, having a life span of 10 to 15 years or more.

## INTERNET RESOURCES

http://www.animalnetwork.com/critters/profiles/chinchilla/default.asp
  "Critters USA On-Line: Critter Collection: Chinchilla"

http://www.chin.buffnet.net/chin_faq.html "The Chinchilla FAQ, version 3"

http://www.etc-etc.com/chapman.htm "The M. F. Chapman Story"

http://www.etc-etc.com/feedchin.htm "Feeding Chinchillas"

http://www.intertex.net.users/rzu2u/chinchi.htm "Chinchillas"

# FAST FACTS

| | |
|---|---|
| Scientific name | *Octodon degus* in Family Octodontidae, Order Rodentia |
| Cost | Unknown—few pet stores have degus or have even heard of them. |
| Food | Commercial guinea pig or chinchilla pellets, timothy hay, hay blocks, alfalfa, sweet potatoes, carrots, dandelion greens. Give sunflower seeds and peanuts only as treats. |
| Housing | A wire mesh cage should include a tree branch for climbing, a sleeping box, a water bottle, a dust box for bathing, and pumice stone or a wood block for gnawing. |
| Training | Handle very gently. Pick up degus from underneath or let them walk onto your hand. |
| Special notes | A special permit may be required to keep degus. |

# DEGU

**DO YOU KNOW WHAT** a degu is? If you don't, you're not alone. Most people have never heard of them. Degus have recently been introduced to the pet industry, but many pet stores do not sell them because so little is known about them. People who do keep degus say that they are wonderful pets—interesting, lovable, and fun to play with. Pet owners also say that degus are a great addition to the fast-growing exotic pet industry.

## A DEGU'S LIFE

Degus look like small chinchillas, although their fur is not as thick. They may grow to about 6 inches (15 centimeters) long, plus an extra 4 to 6 inches (10 to 15 centimeters) for the tail, and they weigh about half a pound (0.25 kilogram). Their brownish fur is actually a mixture of brown and black hairs; the more black, the darker the fur. In their native Chile, Peru, Bolivia, and Argentina, degus can be found from lowland areas along the coast up to nearly a mile (about 1.5 kilometers) high in the Andes Mountains. They live in cracks or holes in rocks.

The degu is sometimes called a "rock rat" or "brush-tail rat," although it is not a rat and is more closely related to chinchillas. The degu is about the size of a rat and has a long tail like a rat's, but its tail has a little "brush" or tuft of hair at the tip (like a gerbil's tail), which it raises slightly when it is walking. Some people think degus look like squirrels, and their behavior is rather squirrellike; they scamper around and climb a lot, and they store food supplies in their burrows.

Degus are very sociable animals. In the wild, they live in large groups or colonies that may include ten to hundreds of animals. Males will fight to defend their home territories. They dig burrows with very complex, extensive tunnels and several

> ### DID YOU KNOW?
> Degus are rodents belonging to the family Octodontidae. *Octodon* refers to the worn enamel on the surface of their teeth, which forms a pattern shaped like a figure eight. A healthy degu's teeth are bright orange or yellow.

> ### DID YOU KNOW?
> A degu's tail will come off when it is grabbed, like a lizard's tail. But unlike a lizard, the degu can use this defensive trick only once; its tail will not grow back. So never grab a degu by the tail.

entrances. They collect dirt, twigs, rocks, and other things lying around and pile them up in mounds near the burrow entrances.

Degus have a well-defined social structure within their groups. Each male's social status is based on the size of the mound outside the entrance to his burrow. The high-ranking degus have the highest mounds. If a mound is accidentally destroyed, however, the owner will lose his high-ranking status.

Degus live in very close-knit families. They are very affectionate to one another and may spend some time resting close together and nuzzling each other's fur. The males also help in raising the young.

Degus use a variety of sounds to communicate with each other. A happy degu will make a warbling sound that sounds like a bunch of short squeaks made close together at a fast rate. Males may also "sing" this way to get the female's attention during courtship. When degus are excited, they may beat their long tails. An unhappy degu will make chattering sounds, like the noise you make when you tap your top teeth against your bottom teeth really fast. Males may make these sounds when defending their territories. An annoyed degu will make a loud squeak like a mouse or a rat. Degus may make this sound if they are grabbed or startled. They may also give out a loud alarm call when danger approaches to warn other degus to hide.

## DEGUS AS PETS

Degus love attention and companionship. In fact, most breeders suggest buying at least two degus if pet owners cannot spend enough time with their pet. Degus are not solitary animals; a lonely degu may become depressed and ill and may even die. It is best to get degus when they are young. Degus that are raised from a young age and are handled often will be much friendlier than older degus that are not familiar with people.

Degus have good memories. They can recognize sounds and voices. They know their owners and are friendlier to people they know. When degus meet

### *Stay Away From Sweets!*

*Degus have a very strict diet. In their native habitat, they live on various kinds of plant life. Fruit, berries, and other sugar-containing foods do not grow in this area. Over many generations of evolution, degus lost the ability to digest sugar-containing foods. In fact, if they eat too much sugar in captivity, they will develop diabetes. Since degus cannot be given the drugs people with diabetes take to control their condition, a degu with diabetes will not live long. So never give degus fruit or any other sugar-containing food!*

strangers, they will be very cautious. They are not aggressive by nature and will rarely bite a person or another degu, unless they are threatened.

Degus sleep at night and are most active during the early morning and evening. Degus are very lively animals and like to run and jump and climb. They are curious and love to explore. Of course, as rodents, they tend to chew a lot. So they need a large, escape-proof cage, plenty of exercise, and "safe" things to chew on.

Like chinchillas, degus also need to take dust baths to keep their fur healthy.

In the wild, degus have a life span of up to 15 years. But in captivity, they rarely live more than 10 years. Their lives are often shortened by a poor diet or a lack of exercise or companionship. Degus that are given plenty of love and proper care can bring a lot of enjoyment to pet owners.

## INTERNET RESOURCES

http://asylum.sf.ca.us/pub/u/seven/degus.html "Degu (*Octodon degus*) Links"

http://home.worldonline.nl/~hleli/DeguInfo.html "Degu Info" by Heinjan Leliveld, 1995

http://www.blarg.net/~critter/articles/sm_furry/degu.html "Octodonts (Degus)" by Adelheit Stahnke and Hubert Hendrichs from *Grzimek's Encyclopedia*

http://www.blarg.net/~critter/articles/sm_furry/degu2.html "Degus" by Gary & Caroline Dean

http://www.geocities.com/Heartland/Prairie/1568/degus.html "Degus"

http://www.nwlink.com/~pawprint/cc_degu_101.html "Degus 101"

http://www.nwlink.com/~pawprint/cc_degu_doings.html "Degu Doings"

http://www.nwlink.com/~pawprint/cc_degu_tips.html "Tips from Toby: Degus"

# HAMSTER

## FAST FACTS

| | |
|---|---|
| Scientific name | *Mesocricetus auratus* (golden hamster), *Phodopus sungoris campbelli* (dwarf Russian or Campbell's hamster), *Cricetulus griseus* (Chinese hamster); all in Family Cricetidae, Order Rodentia |
| Cost | Under $10 for golden hamsters |
| Food | Commercial hamster food; can also be fed small amounts of fruits and vegetables such as carrots, apples, cabbage, broccoli, pears, dandelion leaves, grapes. |
| Housing | A commercial hamster Habitrail should include compartments for nesting, storing, tunneling. There should also be a sleeping box, a water bottle, exercise wheel, and pumice stone or wood block for gnawing. |
| Training | Always be gentle and use treats to train a hamster to stay on your shoulder or to stand on command. |
| Special notes | Owning hamsters is illegal in some states and in many countries because they can damage crops if they escape. Leave inexperienced mothers undisturbed for a few weeks after they give birth; otherwise they may eat their young. |

# HAMSTER

**HAMSTERS ARE VERY** popular pets. Even if you have never owned one, you probably know someone who has. In fact, millions of people own hamsters all over the world. These rodents make great pets because they are small, cute animals that take up little room, are clean, and are easy to care for. When hamsters are taken care of properly and given plenty of attention, they can become very tame and give hours of enjoyment.

## THE FIRST DOMESTICATED HAMSTERS

Hamsters were first discovered in 1839 in the Syrian desert in the Middle East. But no more were seen in Syria until almost a hundred years later. In 1930, Palestinian zoologist Israel Aharoni went on a field trip to Syria to see if these wild hamsters still existed. Finally, Aharoni and a crew of men dug up a nest with a mother hamster and her litter of eleven babies. These Syrian hamsters were also called golden hamsters because of the color of their fur.

Professor Aharoni brought the mother hamster and her babies back so they could be studied at the Hebrew University in Jerusalem. Soon after they arrived, the mother was killed, and after two separate escapes only four hamsters were left. They settled down in their new surroundings, and about four months after they were taken from their burrow in Syria, a young female gave birth to the first litter of golden hamsters ever born in captivity.

Hamsters are very good breeders. Females are ready to breed at about five weeks and then give birth only sixteen days later. In the laboratory at the university, the hamsters were breeding so well that the researchers soon had more ham-

### Escape Artists

*Hamsters may be cute and cuddly, but you can't take your eyes off them for a second. Hamsters are escape artists; they can squeeze their plump bodies through very skinny places. You'd hardly believe it even if you saw it with your own eyes. A hamster in a cage with bars that are close together can squeeze right out to freedom. The hamster can also get through tiny holes in the walls, with a little help from its sharp teeth. A hamster loose in a house can cause as much trouble as a wild rat or mouse.*

sters than they knew what to do with. Some of the extras were sent to England and France, others to India and Egypt. Finally, in 1938 some golden hamsters were sent to scientists in the United States.

In laboratories all over the world, hamsters lived and multiplied. The scientists who raised them noticed that these little animals became tame and friendly. So some of these scientists took extra hamsters home as pets for their children. Soon word got out about their "pet potential," and pet dealers started to breed them. It wasn't long until golden hamsters became a huge pet craze.

## A HAMSTER'S LIFE

Many different kinds of hamsters live in the wild in Europe, the Middle East, and Asia. All hamsters are rodents. They are constantly gnawing on things, and hamsters in the wild are often considered pests because they dig up the ground and chew up farmers' crops.

Golden hamsters live in deserts and hide out in deep burrows to get away from the hot sun. The hamsters use their sharp claws to dig complex burrows that contain extensive tunnels with compartments for nesting and storing food.

Like squirrels, hamsters store their food. Hamsters have large cheek pouches that go all the way back to their shoulders. They use these cheek pouches to collect and carry food, bedding, and even their newborn babies. The hamster brings the contents in its cheek pouches back to its burrow to unload. Even hamsters in captivity that get plenty to eat have this hoarding behavior. A hamster can carry up to half its body weight in its cheek pouches. The first time you see a hamster with bulging cheeks, you may almost think it has mumps.

## HAMSTERS AS PETS

The golden hamster, also called the Syrian hamster, is the most popular hamster pet all over the world. It is believed that the millions of hamsters in laboratories and homes today all come from the original stock brought back from the wild by Israel Aharoni.

Golden hamsters are small animals with short, stubby tails. Their bodies are about 6 to 7 inches (15 to 18 centimeters) long and weigh about 4 ounces (112 grams). They usually have a golden-colored fur coat, but there are now variations including cinnamon, cream, white, and "teddy bear" (the longhair kind).

Golden hamsters are solitary animals. They do not like to be in the company of other hamsters. Females are more aggressive than males and will fight to the death (unless it is mating time). So hamsters should be housed separately.

Hamsters may bite if they are annoyed, especially if they are awakened when they are sleeping. They are very grumpy when their sleep is disturbed.

Hamsters can be tamed easily when they are young. If they are handled regularly and very gently, they will become very friendly. Hamsters can even be taught to do tricks, especially when they are given a treat like a raisin or peanut. A hamster can be taught to walk on your arm and perch on your shoulder. It can also learn to stand on its hind legs when you say the word *stand* and hold a treat above its head. Hamsters are active animals and need exercise wheels, little ladders to climb, and a tissue roll for tunneling.

A couple of other kinds of hamster pets are becoming increasingly popular. The dwarf Russian, or Campbell's hamster, originally from Siberia, Manchuria, and northern China, can now be found in many pet stores. These dwarf hamsters are very small, about half the size of a golden hamster. Dwarf Russian hamsters are much more sociable than golden hamsters. In the wild, they live in pairs or in small groups; in captivity they are friendly toward people.

Chinese hamsters are also becoming popular pets. They originate from Northern China and Mongolia and belong to a group known as ratlike hamsters. Their tails are the longest of any of the hamsters—up to 4 inches (10 centimeters). Their fur is a mousy gray on top and white on the underparts.

Chinese hamsters started to become popular in the 1970s when the dwarf Russian hamster was introduced to the pet market. But they are not as popular as the dwarf Russian hamsters, probably because of their mouselike appearance and problems in breeding them in captivity. Chinese hamsters can make good pets but are very fast-moving animals and may be difficult to handle.

Hamsters have a very short life span—only 2 to 3 years on the average, although some may live up to 4 years.

> **DID YOU KNOW?**
> Hamsters will hibernate when the temperature gets low or if there is little light.

> **DID YOU KNOW?**
> Hamsters are ground-dwelling animals. They are not climbers. So never leave a pet hamster on a table or some other place where it can fall. Hamsters can hurt themselves or even die if they fall down to the floor.

## INTERNET RESOURCES

http://www.animalnetwork.com/critters/profiles/hamster/default.asp "Critters USA On-Line: Critter Collection: Hamster" by Moira C. Harris

http://www.hamsters.co.uk/camp.htm, http://www.hamsters.co.uk/chin.htm, http://www.hamsters.co.uk/fact3.htm, http://www.hamsters.co.uk/handle.htm, http://www.hamsters.co.uk/intro.htm, http://www.hamsters.co.uk/syrian.htm
Articles by Lorraine Hill, 1997, 1998: "The Dwarf Campbell's Russian Hamster (*Phodopus sungoris campbelli*)," "The Chinese Hamster (*Cricetulus griseus*)," "Hamster Fact Sheet—Syrian Hamsters," "Handling," "Introduction to Hamsters," "The Syrian Hamsters (*Mesocricetus auratus*)"

# GERBIL

## FAST FACTS

| | |
|---|---|
| Scientific name | *Meriones unguiculatus* (Mongolian gerbil) in Family Cricetidae, Subfamily Gerbillinae, Order Rodentia |
| Cost | Under $10 |
| Food | Commercial hamster or gerbil food; can also be fed small amounts of fruits and vegetables such as carrots, apples, cabbage, broccoli, pears, dandelion leaves, grapes. |
| Housing | A commercial hamster or gerbil Habitrail should include compartments for nesting, storing, tunneling. Also needed are a sleeping box, water bottle, exercise wheel, and pumice stone or wood block for gnawing. |
| Training | Always be gentle and use treats to train gerbils to stay on a shoulder or to stand. |
| Special notes | Owning gerbils is illegal in some states and in many countries because they may damage crops if they escape. |

# GERBIL

People sometimes confuse hamsters and gerbils. They are both small rodents that make great pets. But these adorable animals look quite different and have different behaviors.

The gerbils' very friendly nature has earned them the nickname "gentle gerbils." They made their way into the pet market about twenty years after hamsters. Since then, gerbil pets have grown ever more popular, becoming almost as common as their hamster cousins.

## THE ORIGIN OF PET GERBILS

Today's pet gerbils are descended from gerbils captured in eastern Mongolia in 1935 by Japanese scientists. Twenty pairs were taken to Japan for laboratory research on various diseases. The gerbils bred very well in captivity, and they made good research subjects.

In America, biologist Victor Schwentker became very interested in these remarkable rodents and requested some gerbils for his scientific research. In 1954 a Japanese laboratory sent over eleven pairs of Mongolian gerbils to a breeding facility in the United States called Tumblebrook Farm.

The technicians at Tumblebrook Farm were surprised to find how friendly and tame these new animals were. The gerbils thrived and multiplied until there were plenty of gentle gerbils to spare. So scientists and technicians started taking gerbils home for pets. Before long, these gerbil owners had enough to give to friends and neighbors. Soon gerbils spread throughout the country, both in scientific laboratories and as pets in people's homes. Pet shops began to stock them, and thus a new pet craze was born.

### The Friendliest Rodents

*Gerbils are probably the friendliest of all rodents. They are almost fearless. While most rodents quickly scurry away and hide when you open their cage, gerbils are more curious. They will come to the cage door and smell around to check out the situation. Gerbils are desert animals; perhaps their fearless behavior comes from the fact that few predators lurk in the barren desert.*

# A GERBIL'S LIFE

Gerbils can be found in the dry desert regions of eastern Europe, Asia, and Africa. They use their long, sharp claws to dig complex underground burrows, complete with many mazelike tunnels with several entrances and rooms for storing food. During the hottest parts of the day, they stay in their burrows to hide from the sun.

An adult gerbil is bigger than a mouse but smaller than a rat. Its fur may be grayish or a tawny brown color. Its body is about 4 inches (10 centimeters) long, plus a tail of the same length. Unlike a rat or mouse tail, a gerbil's long tail is covered completely with hair and has a tuft of hair at the tip. (The loose skin from the end of the tail will be stripped off if it is grabbed by a predator, and the lost part will not grow back.) The gerbil uses its tail for balance, especially when it stands up on its hind legs. Its hind legs are long and strong, and it can jump like a kangaroo. Gerbils also stomp their hind feet to communicate with others when they are annoyed, as a warning of danger, or during mating.

## GERBILS AS PETS

The Mongolian gerbil is the only gerbil that is widely sold as a pet in the United States. Gerbils make great pets because they are friendly, clean, and fun to play with. They rarely bite, unless they are really annoyed. They are active in the daytime but take frequent rests or naps.

Because of their very sociable nature, gerbils should be kept in pairs (either a breeding pair or two females or males) or in groups, rather than singly. It is best to get two gerbils from the same group, or to pair them soon after they are weaned. Adults may fight with strangers.

Gerbils are very clean animals and they are practically odorless. Being desert animals, they drink little water, getting most of their water from moisture in the foods they eat. As a result, they make only a few drops of urine, and their feces are dry. So cleaning the gerbils' cage is a really easy and not very smelly job.

If your pet gerbil is startled or frightened, it may quickly drop to the ground. Don't worry—it may be playing dead. In the wild, gerbils may use this trick to escape from predators. After the danger has passed, the gerbil will quickly get up and dart away.

Gerbils should never be left on tabletops or other furniture. They are wonderful jumpers, covering up to several feet in a single bound, but they can really hurt themselves if they fall to the ground.

Like hamsters, gerbils can be taught to do some tricks, using treats like sunflower seeds as rewards. Your pet gerbil can learn to stay on your shoulder or stand up on its hind legs as you wave a treat above its head. Gerbils are more active than hamsters and should have an exercise wheel, ladders, or blocks.

Gerbils live slightly longer than hamsters—up to 4 to 5 years.

**DID YOU KNOW?**
Unlike many other rodents, gerbils mate for life. If the mate dies, the survivor may not accept another mate right away.

## INTERNET RESOURCES

**http://members.aol.com/zerogvty/GERBIL.HTM** "Zero's Pets—Gerbils" (photos and a video)

**http://users.bart.nl/~fredveen/gerbiluk.htm** "Gerbil Information Page"

**http://www12.geocities.com/RainForest/1584/gerbils.htm** "Gerbils"

**http://www.cvm.uiuc.edu/ceps/petcolumns/gerbils.htm** "Pet Gerbil Care" by Theresa A. Fuess, Ph.D.

**http://www.orst.edu/instruct/ans280/gerbil.htm** "Gerbils"

**http://www.rodent.demon.co.uk/gerbils/gerbfaq.htm** "Gerbil FAQ" by Michelle and Kirk Haines (very extensive information)

**http://www.rodent.demon.co.uk/gerbils/links.htm** "Gerbil Links" (to information and fun)

**http://www.webcom.com/~lstead/rodents/gerbils/html** "Mongolian Gerbils as Pets" by Lewis Stead

# DUPRASI

# FAST FACTS

| | |
|---|---|
| Scientific name | *Pachyuromys duprasis* in Family Gerbillinae, Order Rodentia |
| Cost | May cost $20 to $30 or more |
| Food | In the wild, they eat leaves, seeds, and insects. As pets, they can eat commercial gerbil food, alfalfa hay, rodent block, and mealworms. Also include fruits and vegetables such as apples, pears, sweet potatoes, carrots, romaine lettuce. Calcium supplements are also necessary. |
| Housing | A 10-gallon (38-liter) or larger aquarium. Should include a thick layer of nesting material (aspen shavings, *not* cedar), sleeping box, water bottle, exercise wheel, dust bath, and pumice stone or wood block for gnawing. |
| Training | Docile and lacking curiosity, the duprasi is mainly a cuddly lap pet rather than a performer. |
| Special notes | Owning a duprasi may be illegal in some states. |

# DUPRASI

HOW WOULD YOU LIKE a plump little rodent that looks like a hamster but has the calm, friendly manner of a gerbil? Then, how about a duprasi? The duprasi is one of the newest exotic animals on the U.S. pet market. These pets are so new that very little information is available on them, and few people even know what they are.

So, what is a duprasi? It is a cute little rodent that belongs to the gerbil family. It is also commonly called the "fat-tailed gerbil."

Like the Mongolian gerbil, the duprasi is friendly and easy to handle. But the duprasi is not closely related to the Mongolian gerbil. These two "gerbils" are different in many ways in their appearance and behavior.

## THE DUPRASI'S LIFE

The duprasi can be found in the dry North Sahara Desert regions of Egypt and Morocco. Duprasi live in deep underground burrows to protect themselves from the hot sun. Duprasi are champion burrowers. Their burrows have different chambers for storing food and nesting. They feed on leaves, seeds, and insects.

The duprasi looks like a cross between a hamster and a gerbil. Its body is chunky like a hamster's but smaller in size like a gerbil's, measuring about 4 inches (10 centimeters) long, with a 2-inch (5-centimeter) fat, lightly furred tail. The duprasi's fur is unlike a hamster's or gerbil's, though. Its tan or gray fur is thick and silky, very similar to the texture of a chinchilla's fur coat. The fluffy fur makes a duprasi look larger than it really is.

### DID YOU KNOW?

The most interesting thing about the duprasi is its tail. As its name suggests, the fat-tailed gerbil has a fat, club-shaped tail that is covered with tiny hairs, something like peach fuzz. The duprasi stores fat reserves and water in its tail. You can see how healthy a duprasi is by looking at its tail. When the animal is in good health or gaining weight, it stores most of its fat in its tail rather than its body. Usually the bigger the tail, the healthier the animal.

The duprasi's fat-tail trait is an important adaptation that has helped it survive in its native habitat, the dry, barren desert. A nursing mother's tail shrinks as she uses up her fat reserves, but as soon as the babies are weaned her tail quickly gets fat again.

The duprasi is considered a diurnal animal—active during the day and sleeping at night. Actually, they are active throughout the day and night. They are active for very short periods between longer periods of sleep.

Duprasi are very social animals. They may live in colonies, with many duprasi living in a small area and each having its own burrow; or they may form communities in which small groups share the same living quarters. Although they are sociable, they are also very territorial, especially the females. Though it is not likely, they may fight.

Duprasi have scent glands on their bellies and rub them on the ground to mark their territories. (Humans can't smell the scent these glands produce.)

## DUPRASI AS PETS

The duprasi's friendly nature makes them good pets. They are easy to handle and rarely bite. Unfortunately, most of those that are available are imported and not easy to get. These small rodents are just starting to be bred in captivity, so it may be some time before they become widely popular.

Because of their social nature, duprasi are happiest when they are kept in pairs (a male and a female or two of the same sex). As with most pets, it is easiest to tame a duprasi pet when it is young. Also, several duprasi get along best when they are introduced at a young age.

Duprasi are not as active as Mongolian gerbils. In fact, duprasi sleep a great deal. During the naps they take between their short periods of activity, they sleep very deeply. You could actually pick up a sleeping duprasi and it still would not wake up right away. You might have to wait a moment for it to wake up. But duprasi are not likely to get upset the way hamsters do when they are awakened suddenly.

Burrowing animals can afford the luxury of sleeping deeply, since they spend their sleep time safe in a cozy burrow. Pet duprasi like to nap in a nest box lined with shredded paper, or in a burrow they dig in the wood shavings that line their cage. (If you attach their tank to an ant farm type of setup, you can see the burrows they dig and peek in at them while they are digging or resting.)

Duprasi will sometimes run on exercise wheels, even though they are often clumsy and slow-moving. But since they are territorial, they run alone; one of them will chase the other away.

A duprasi that is well cared for will live up to 5 years.

**INTERNET RESOURCES**
http://users.bart.nl/~fredveen/otherduprasiuk.htm *"Pachyuromys duprasis"*

**http://www.animalnetwork.com/critters/profiles/duprasi/default.asp** "Critters USA On-Line: Critter Collection: Duprasi" by Helen Moreno

**http://www.intertex.net/users/rzu2u/duprasi.htm** "Duprasi: Get to Know the Fat-tailed Gerbil"

**http://www.rodent.demon.co.uk/gerbils/duprasi.htm** "Duprasi or Fat-Tailed Gerbils" by Julian Barker

**http://www.webcom.com/lstead/rodents/duprasi.html** "Duprasi FAQ" by Lewis Stead, 1996

## FAST FACTS

| | |
|---|---|
| Scientific name | *Rattus norvegicus* (Norway rat) in Family Muridae, Order Rodentia; *Cricetomys gambianus* (giant African pouched rat) |
| Cost | Under $10 |
| Food | Commercial rat or mouse food; can also be fed fruits and vegetables including broccoli, kale, sweet potatoes, kidney beans, grapes, cherries, bananas, apples, melons, oranges. |
| Housing | Large cage or aquarium with bedding (aspen shavings). Needs sleeping box, food dish, water bottle, large exercise wheel, and pumice stone or wood block for gnawing. |
| Training | Always be gentle and use treats when training rats. They can be taught to come when called by name, ride on your shoulder or in a pocket, and play games with owner. |
| Special notes | Owning rats may be illegal in some areas. |

# RAT

MANY PEOPLE ARE AFRAID of rats. These rodents have a bad reputation as dirty, mean, and disease-carrying. This may be true of a rat from the sewer. But the rats bred as pets are very different from wild rats. Tame rats are friendly, smart, and lovable animals, and they make great pets. Pet owners say that their rats are a lot of fun, and that they are just as smart as dogs.

## THE DOMESTICATION OF THE RAT

No one is quite sure where and when rats were first domesticated. It may have happened during the nineteenth century, when rat killing was a popular sporting event. In matches held in London pubs, people placed bets on whose dog could kill the most rats in the shortest amount of time. It is believed that the people who supplied the rats must have caught albinos (white rats with pink eyes) from time to time. These albinos, produced by accidental genetic changes in the wild rat population, were objects of curiosity. So some albino rats were probably kept and bred, and they became the ancestors of today's domesticated rats.

**DID YOU KNOW?**
Only seven of the approximately eighty species of rats really deserve their bad reputation as dirty, destructive, disease-carrying rodents.

These pet rats are variations of a species called the brown rat, or Norway rat. (Actually, they came originally from central Asia, not Norway. They got their name from the fact that they first spread to England in the early eighteenth cen-

### The Laboratory Rat

*So many rats have been used in laboratory experiments that "lab rat" has become a synonym for an experimental subject. Medical researchers use domesticated rats (mainly the albinos) in studies of disease, drug effects, heredity, and nutrition. Rats' intelligence has also made them popular subjects in studies of learning and other aspects of behavior. For example, rats quickly learn to find their way around a maze when they are periodically given treats as rewards. They can also learn to push down levers when they know they will be rewarded for the effort.*

tury as stowaways on a Norwegian ship.) Norway rats are destructive pests wherever they go, living in homes and other buildings and eating or fouling food, clothing, and other goods. They migrated to North America from Europe around 1775 by stowing away on ships or in people's luggage.

Wild Norway rats are very aggressive and may bite humans who get in their way. The domesticated albino rats that were bred from them, however, are much less skittish and aggressive. In fact, when handled gently and often from an early age, they become quite gentle and friendly to humans. These rats have been selectively bred for their calm nature, and they rarely bite. They are clean and do not transmit diseases to people.

## RATS AS PETS

Rats bond to their owners in much the same way that dogs do. Like dogs, rats love attention, they love to play, and they can be taught to do tricks.

After more than a hundred years of selective breeding, tame rats come in a wide variety of colors including white, blue, lilac, chocolate, amber, mink, pearl, champagne, fawn, cinnamon, black, beige, and agouti (wild color). The rat looks like a mouse, but it is much larger. The rat grows to about 8 to 10 inches (20 to 25 centimeters) long, with a 6- to 8-inch (15- to 20-centimeter) naked tail. An adult rat may weigh from 9 to 23 ounces (250 to 660 grams), about ten times as much as a mouse.

Rats are the most intelligent of all the rodents. They have amazing memories and can learn to do many different things. You can teach your pet rat to come when you call it by name. It can also learn how to walk on a tiny leash. Rats love to walk through the grass and explore. Rats are also smart enough to play games with their owners, such as tag, hide-and-seek, tug-of-war, and peek-a-boo. Rats will wrestle with your hand or chase a string, just like a kitten.

Rats love to ride on your shoulder so they can look around. You can also let your rat ride in a fanny pack or in your shirt pocket. Rats should not be allowed to run loose in your house, though, unless you keep a close eye on them. Since rats are rodents, they can do a lot of damage to electrical cords, furniture, and other items. You can teach them to stay on furniture, beds, or tabletops rather than running around on the floor if they are restricted to these places when they are young. When they get older, they will not want to get down on the floor (although some rats are born explorers.)

Rats are social creatures by nature. In the wild, they live in large family groups. Therefore, as pets, rats thrive on companionship. You need to handle your pet rat as much as possible to gain its trust. (Treats can help make it feel friendly.)

### DID YOU KNOW?

Because rats are so intelligent, they get bored a lot more easily than other rodents, such as hamsters and gerbils. They love to explore and check things out. But that could mean trouble. Rats may get into things that could be harmful.

> ## Giant African Pouched Rat
>
> *The giant African pouched rat makes a very interesting pet. These rats are very large—as much as 10 to 17 inches (25 to 43 centimeters) long from the head to the base of the tail. The tail may be the same length or longer! They may weigh from 2 to 6 pounds (1 to 3 kilograms).*
>
> *These rats are a different species from the common Norway rats. They are named for their cheek pouches, in which, like hamsters, they carry food. They may also collect and carry items, such as buttons, coins, or other small objects.*
>
> *Giant African pouched rats are shy but very affectionate and will easily bond with their owners. They can live up to 8 years, longer than most other rats.*

Many breeders say, however, that no matter how much time you spend with your pet, rats also need to be with their own species. So you should keep more than one pet rat.

Some people fear that rats will become less friendly to their owners when they are kept in a group. That is not true. In fact, rats that are kept in groups are just as affectionate as single rats, as long as all the rats are handled frequently. Rats get along better with others of their species when they are introduced at a young age, however.

Both males and females make good pets. But females tend to be more active than males and rarely enjoy being held for long periods of time. Males get larger and heavier than females, and they tend to make better lap pets.

Keeping pet rats can be a rewarding experience if you can handle the responsibility. But like many other rodents, rats have a short life span of only 2 to 3 years, although some may live up to 6 years.

## INTERNET RESOURCES

**http://freezone.com/kclub/purfpets/rats.html** "Pet Rats"

**http://www.animalnetwork.com/critters/profiles/rat/default.asp** "Critters USA On-Line: Critter Collection: Rational Rats"

**http://www.ndirect.co.uk/~lscmrc/ratas.htm** "Rats as Pets" by Elaine Johnstone

**http://www.rmca.org/second.htm** Home page of the Rat and Mouse Club of America (links, resources, and articles from the magazine *Rat and Mouse Gazette*)

**http://www.rmca.org/Resources/apair.txt** "Why Rats Need Company" by Angela Horn

**http://www.rmca.org/Resources/petrats.txt** "Pet Rat Information Sheet" by A. Swierzy and A. Horn, 1997

**http://www.webcom/lstead/rodents/rats.html** "Rats" by Lewis Stead

**http://www.blarg.net/~critter/articles/sm_furry/rat2.html** "African Giant Pouched Rats as Pets" by Lynn Smallwood

**http://www.intertex.net/users/rzu2u/gambian.htm** "Giant African Pouched Rat"

## FAST FACTS

| | |
|---|---|
| Scientific name | *Mus musculus* (house mouse) in Family Muridae, Order Rodentia; *Graphiurs murinus* in Family Gliridae (African pygmy dormouse), Order Rodentia; *Mus minutoides* in Family Muridae (African pygmy mouse) |
| Cost | Under $2 (house mice) |
| Food | Commercial mice food; can also be fed fruits and vegetables including broccoli, kale, sweet potatoes, kidney beans, grapes, cherries, bananas, apples, melons, and oranges. |
| Housing | Large cage or aquarium with bedding (aspen shavings). Needs a sleeping box, food dish, water bottle, large exercise wheel, ladder, rope, and pumice stone or wood block for gnawing. |
| Training | Always be gentle and use treats when training mice. |
| Special notes | Owning mice may be illegal in some areas. |

# MOUSE

**"EEEK, A MOUSE!"** It seems funny to imagine someone jumping up on a chair while a tiny mouse scurries across the floor. Why are people afraid of a creature that is so small and looks rather harmless? Actually, like their much larger rodent relatives, rats, mice can cause some real problems. Mice eat and spoil stored food supplies, damage clothing and other goods, and they also carry diseases.

Mice can certainly be dreadful pests; they can also make great pets. Pet mice are not quite the same as the mice you hear under the floorboards in your house, or the ones that scurry through fields in the wild. The mice you find in pet stores are tame, and they are not only cute but very smart, gentle, and playful, as well.

## THE DOMESTICATION OF MICE

House mice are one of the oldest domesticated mammals on Earth. About ten thousand years ago, when people in Asia first found out how to grow crops and store grain, mice of this species, which lived in the area, left their home in the wild and moved into people's houses to share their shelter and food. When people migrated into new areas, they unintentionally carried house mice along with them hidden in packs of clothes or food, or hitching rides in boats. Gradually, house mice spread all over Europe, Africa, and Asia.

These mice quickly became pests. Typical rodents, they gnawed on wood structures inside the walls, floors, and ceilings in people's homes. Mice also fed on scraps of food that people dropped or threw away, and they ruined a great deal of the food and grain supply. In some places, such as Greece, it was noticed that certain diseases occurred where mice were plentiful.

By the twelfth century, China was breeding some of these house pests into house pets. Meanwhile, people—and house mice—continued to spread to other parts of the world. By the 1500s, Old World house mice had been carried to North and South America by English, French, and Spanish ships.

Today's pet mice are direct descendants of the house pets that were first domesticated in China.

## MICE IN THE WILD

There are still wild strains of house mice that live in the Old World. These mice are burrowing animals. They live in a branching network of tunnels that are dug out in fields where plant cover and food are readily available. Each family has its own nest with one male mouse, his mate (or sometimes two mates), and their young. Tunnels connect the nest with other nests and with community eating places, storage burrows, areas for urination and defecation, and escape holes.

In the mouse community, mice visit other families and get together for grooming and socializing. The males fight to establish their place in the social structure and to win the right to a nest and a mate. Females do not take part in this but will fight to defend their babies against intruders. All the mice in the community will defend their home territory against invading mice from other burrows.

## MICE AS PETS

Wild mice can be very nasty and do not make good pets. Tame mice, however, are very gentle, playful animals. White mice are the most common pet mice, but there is a wide variety of colors including black, brown, tan, and two-toned combinations. "Fancy mice" have been specially bred for competition in pet shows, with standards just as strict as those set for purebred dogs. ("Fancy" is used in its old sense, meaning "hobby.") Some fancy mice have extraordinarily silky fur with color varieties including chocolate, cinnamon, champagne, coffee, and Siamese. Others have curly hair, or no hair at all! Fancy mice have also been selectively bred for calm and friendly behavior. Many of the mice sold in pet stores, however, have been bred as snake food, rather than as pets, so they have not been chosen for health or temperament.

Since mice are social animals by nature, they should not be housed alone. Mice are not likely to play with you the way rats will, but they are very entertaining to watch. Mice do play with each other, and with toys like ladders or ropes that they can climb. They can also run through mazes.

African pygmy mice are another species kept as pets. They are smaller cousins of the common pet mouse. In fact, they are the smallest living rodent. African pygmy mice have a body length of only 1.5 to 3 inches (about 4 to 8 centimeters), with another inch or two (3 to 5 centimeters) of tail, and weigh less than one-quarter of an ounce (7 grams). These are not exactly "lap pets" because they are very active animals and can jump amazing distances.

## INTERNET RESOURCES

http://www.animalnetwork.com/critters/profiles/mouse/default.asp "Critters USA On-Line: Critter Collection: Mouse" by Tina Bolton

http://www.rmca.org/Resources/mouse-faq.txt "Pet Mouse FAQ" by Angela Horn, 1997

http://www.webcom/lstead/rodents/mice.html "Mice as Pets" by Lewis Stead, 1996

http://Members.aol.com/drdoolitel/Pygmy.htm "African Pygmy Mice"

http://www.nwlink.com/~pawprint/cc_pygmy.html "Pygmy Mice"

http://www.animalnetwork.com/critters/profiles/dormouse/default.asp "Critters USA On-Line: Critter Connection: Dormouse" by Stephanie C. Ostveen

http://Members.aol.com/drdoolitel/Dormouse.htm "African Pygmy Dormouse"

## FAST FACTS

| | |
|---|---|
| Scientific name | *Glaucomys volans* in Subfamily Petauristinae, Family Sciuridae (Squirrel family), Order Rodentia |
| Cost | May cost $75 to $80, but mail-order may cost up to $200 |
| Food | Diet should include seeds, nuts, and mealworms. Also include fruits and vegetables such as apples, melons, clover, alfalfa, carrots, and romaine lettuce. Pecans make good treats. Calcium supplements are also necessary. |
| Housing | Birdcages are good since the squirrels like to climb. Cage should include nesting material (pine shavings, crumpled paper towels), sleeping box, water dish, food dish, exercise wheel, and fresh tree branches. |
| Training | Can learn how to stay in your pocket and glide onto your shoulder from a high perch. |
| Special notes | Owning a flying squirrel may be illegal in some states. |

# FLYING SQUIRREL

**A RODENT THAT FLIES?** Actually, flying squirrels don't quite live up to their name. They should really be called "gliding squirrels" because that's what they do—they glide through the air like animated furry kites.

In some ways, flying squirrels are perfect pocket pets. They are very gentle animals and love to crawl into a nice warm shirt pocket to be close to their owners. Flying squirrels are adorable, fun, and affectionate. But unlike a hamster or a guinea pig, which take up very little room, flying squirrels need plenty of room to play, especially when they glide.

## GLIDING THROUGH THE AIR

What an amazing thing it is to watch a flying squirrel glide through the air. These little rodents do not have wings. Instead, they have a gliding membrane, or patagium, which is a furry fold of skin that stretches from wrist to ankle. When the flying squirrel stretches out its front and back legs, the fold of skin forms a wing-like surface. Flying squirrels always glide from a high place on a tree to a lower place on another tree.

When the flying squirrel is ready to glide, it will climb to the top of a tree. It bobs its head to the left and then to the right, as if it is trying to judge the distance. Then it launches itself into the air with its legs spread so that the membrane is stretched out. The squirrel uses its furry, flattened tail to guide its "flight." The tail helps to control both the speed and the direction. The squirrel can maneuver around tree branches and other obstacles. When it is ready to land, its tail flips up, and its arms and legs swing forward, forming a sort of parachute that helps it to slow down. The squirrel then lands upright on the tree. Flying squirrels can glide up to 150 feet (46 meters) or more.

> **DID YOU KNOW?**
> Flying squirrels are not really "new" pets. They have been kept as pets for hundreds of years.

## A FLYING SQUIRREL'S LIFE

Two kinds of flying squirrels live in North America: northern flying squirrels and southern flying squirrels. Only the southern flying squirrels are sold as pets. In the wild, southern flying squirrels can be found in southeastern Canada, the eastern United States (as well as Nebraska), Mexico, and even as far south as Honduras. Northern flying squirrels, found only in Canada and the northern United States, are much rarer, and, in fact, subspecies are officially listed as endangered.

The southern flying squirrel is grayish brown and weighs no more than 4 ounces (113 grams). Its body is about 5 to 6 inches (13 to 15 centimeters) long, with a 3- to 4-inch (8- to 10-centimeter) tail. The flying squirrel's tail is flat and furry like a feather, rather than round and bushy like that of other tree squirrels.

Flying squirrels make their homes in the hollows of trees. They travel by climbing up and down trees and gliding from one tree to the next. They are very awkward on the ground.

Flying squirrels are social animals, especially in the winter. They do not hibernate, but many squirrels snuggle up together in a single nest to keep each other warm against the bitter-cold winter temperatures.

Flying squirrels communicate with a variety of high-pitched sounds. Their usual call may be *chuck-chuck-chuck*. When they are annoyed or alarmed, they may make squealing sounds. At other times, they make chirping sounds.

Flying squirrels are not strongly territorial, but females may defend their territories at certain times of the year. The home ranges of females do not overlap with those of other females. Males are not very territorial, and their home ranges often overlap with those of other males.

## FLYING SQUIRRELS AS PETS

Flying squirrels that are hand-raised from a young age make wonderful pets. They are friendly and affectionate. The flying squirrel can learn to stay in your warm, comforting pocket during the day, while you do your daily activities. Some pet owners say that flying squirrels may glide from one person to another or from a high perch to a person's shoulder.

### Night Flights

*Unlike other tree squirrels, flying squirrels are nocturnal animals—they are active at night and sleep during the day. They have really large, dark eyes that help them to see at night, especially when they are gliding. Their nighttime habits explain why few people have ever seen one in the wild, even though they are believed to be as common as gray squirrels.*

Since flying squirrels are nocturnal animals, they may make a lot of noise at night—vocalizing, climbing, or chewing in their cage. Some people say that they have gotten used to it. Some flying squirrel owners let their pet out at night to run loose in the house while they are sleeping. This can be disastrous, however. Flying squirrels can get into a lot of trouble if they are not watched. They are very curious and will check out every nook and cranny, and they could get hurt. Also, since they are rodents, they love to chew, and that includes electrical wires and other things in the house.

Flying squirrels that are well cared for can have a life span of up to 15 years.

## INTERNET RESOURCES

**http://www.acmepet.com/exotic/library/flysqfaq.html** "Flying Squirrel FAQ by Tom Slattery

**http://www.animalnetwork.com/critters/profiles/flyingsquirrel/default.asp** "Critters USA On-Line: Critter Collection: Southern Flying Squirrels"

**http://www.blarg.net/~critter/articles/sm_furry/flsqurl1.html** "Adorable Flying Squirrels" by Curt Howard

**http://www.dc-adnet.com/wrl/southern.htm** "Southern Flying Squirrels"

**http://www.homearts.com/depts/pastime/a7squib1.frm** "What Is a Flying Squirrel, Anyway?"

**http://www.homearts.com/depts/pastime/a7squib2.frm** "Flying Squirrels—Pros"

**http://www.homearts.com/depts/pastime/a7squib3.frm** "Flying Squirrels—Cons"

**http://www.intertex.net/users/rzu2u/flysqrl.htm** "Flying Squirrels"

**http://www.ngpc.state.ne.us/wildlife/flysqu.html** "Southern Flying Squirrel"

# GUINEA PIG

# FAST FACTS

| | |
|---|---|
| Scientific name | *Cavia porcellus* in Family Caviidae, Order Rodentia |
| Cost | About $15 and up |
| Food | Commercial guinea pig food, hay, lettuce, celery, dandelion leaves, grass clippings; also fruits and vegetables such as carrots, apples, cabbage, broccoli |
| Housing | Wire cage or wooden hutch with compartments for sleeping and feeding. Should include bedding (aspen shavings), sleeping box, water bottle, food dish, and pumice stone or wood block for gnawing. |
| Training | Always be gentle and use treats to train guinea pigs to feed from your hand and do simple tricks. |
| Special notes | If a female guinea pig is bred for the first time after the age of 6 months, her litter will have to be delivered surgically by a veterinarian. |

# GUINEA PIG

GUINEA PIGS ARE AMONG the most lovable of all the rodent pets. A guinea pig will plop down on your lap or on your bed and just sit there for long periods of time. It doesn't get cranky the way a hamster sometimes does, and it won't squirm out of your hands like a gerbil. Guinea pigs are somewhat larger than their rodent relatives—hamsters, gerbils, and mice—which makes them a lot easier to handle.

Guinea pigs are popular pets all over the world because they are adorable, gentle, and they make great companions.

> ### DID YOU KNOW?
> Guinea pigs have been so useful in laboratory research that anyone who takes part in an experiment or tries something for the first time is called a "guinea pig."

## THE DOMESTICATION OF THE GUINEA PIG

In the 1500s when Spanish armies conquered South America, they found that many of the natives were keeping cute little animals as pets and for food. The Spaniards had never seen anything like them. They were the descendants of wild cavies that had been tamed by the Inca Indians of Peru. These small, plump animals were timid and gentle, and easy to raise and keep. The tame cavies were so important to the ancient Inca that they buried these little animals in the tombs of their kings and nobles.

In the years that followed the Spanish conquest, returning conquerors, and later traders who stopped at South America, took cavies home with them. These animals began to be called guinea pigs, and now they can be found on every continent.

## A GUINEA PIG'S LIFE

In the wild, guinea pigs can be found in the grassy plains of South America, on the edges of forests, in marshes, and in rocky areas. They find shelter in dense grasses or dig burrows in soil or among rocks to hide from the hot sun during the day. Guinea pigs are nocturnal animals and go out at night in search of food. They are vegetarians, feeding on grasses, leaves, grains, and fruits. Wild cavies live in family groups of five to ten or more animals. They communicate with each other in high-pitched squeaks and squeals.

## GUINEA PIGS AS PETS

The wild cavies that the Inca tamed in Peru many centuries ago had short, coarse fur that was usually gray or reddish brown. This type of fur is called agouti. Domesticated guinea pigs now come in many color variations and patterns, such as orange, black-and-white "belted," and tricolor. Most are shorthaired, but some have long, straight, silky hair that makes them look like a floor mop. Others have hair that grows in many curly cowlicks all over their body.

**DID YOU KNOW?**
Cavies need to eat their vegetables every day. They are the only mammals besides primates that cannot produce their own vitamin C, which is supplied in foods like fruits and vegetables.

Guinea pigs are small and chunky. They grow to about 10 to 14 inches (25 to 36 centimeters) long, and they weigh about 1 to 3 pounds (0.5 to 1.4 kilograms) when they are full grown. Although guinea pigs are rodents, they do not have a long, pointed snout like their smaller rodent relatives, such as rats and mice. A guinea pig's snout is much shorter and blunter. Also, unlike most rodents, the guinea pig does not have any tail at all. It does have some small tailbones at the end of the spine, but these do not show on the outside.

Guinea pigs are very gentle animals, but they need to be handled regularly to become really tame. You can train your guinea pig to feed out of your hand.

After a while, you'll know when your pet is hungry because it will start to beg eagerly for food by squeaking and sitting up on its hind legs.

You won't have much trouble finding your guinea pig if it escapes. Guinea pigs are poor climbers, and they are too large to slip through cracks—so they don't have as many places to hide as hamsters, gerbils, and mice.

Guinea pigs need plenty of exercise. It would be ideal to put your pet in a fenced-in area so it can explore. Or just keep an eye on it if you take it outside. Guinea pigs can also be kept in outdoor hutches as long as the weather is warm. Since their native habitat is in a warm climate, they cannot tolerate cool temperatures. They stay healthiest in places where the temperature is above 65°F (18°C).

A single pet guinea pig can be content if it receives a lot of attention from its owner. But since these are sociable animals, they get along well in pairs (two of the same sex, or a male and a female) or groups. Having animal companions does not make them any less cuddly and attentive to their owners. Pet guinea pigs can live from 5 to 8 years.

## INTERNET RESOURCES

**http://members.aol.com/cdalziel/cavie.htm** "The Guinea Pig Page" by Colin and Alison Dalziel

**http://www12.geocities.com/RainForest/1584/guineapigs.htm** "Guinea Pigs"

**http://www.aracnet.com/~seagull/Guineas/#Intro** "Seagull's Guinea Pig Compendium"

**http://www.bcyellowpages.com/advert/b/BCHES/guinea.htm** "Guinea Pig Care"

**http://www.halcyon.com/integra/drdeeb.html** "Dr. Barb Deeb's Guide to Guinea Pig Care"

**http://www.meerschweinchen.ch/en/eallgeme.htm** "Guinea Pigs: General"

**http://www.soft.net.uk/trilo/guinea.htm** "Caviidae (Guinea Pigs)"

## F A S T   F A C T S

| | |
|---|---|
| Scientific name | *Oryctolagus cuniculus* in Family Leporidae, Order Lagomorpha |
| Cost | $7 to $30 and up |
| Food | Commercial rabbit pellets, alfalfa hay, lettuce, carrots, cabbage, dandelion leaves; avoid starchy foods such as bread or cookies. |
| Housing | Metal or wooden hutch with compartments for sleeping and feeding. Should include bedding (aspen shavings), sleeping box, water bottle, food dish, and pumice stone or wood block for gnawing. |
| Training | Like cats, rabbits can be trained to go in a litter box. |
| Special notes | Females should be spayed if they are not going to be bred, to avoid later development of uterine cancer. |

# RABBIT

A BUNNY RABBIT MIGHT sound like the perfect gift for Easter. But then that adorable, fluffy Easter rabbit suddenly becomes a big responsibility.

Rabbits are not as easy pets as some people think. They are a bit more sensitive than some other pocket pets and should be handled very carefully. Pet rabbits also need plenty of love and attention to become tame and gentle. Rabbits take a lot of work, but they can be rewarding pets.

## THE DOMESTICATION OF THE RABBIT

People have been raising rabbits for thousands of years. Around 1000 B.C., Phoenician traders picked up some rabbits when they sailed to Spain. They carried these European animals with them to northern Africa and other areas around the Mediterranean. The ancient Romans liked to hunt rabbits and were very fond of their meat. They began to raise rabbits in walled enclosures and took them along to the countries they conquered. Soon rabbits had spread all over Europe. They did so well in some places that they became pests, eating farm crops.

### Not a Rodent!

*For years, it was thought that rabbits were rodents. Like rodents, rabbits have a constant need for gnawing because they have very large, long front teeth that keep growing. But a rabbit's teeth are somewhat different from a rodent's. While rodents have only four front teeth, two on the top and two on the bottom, rabbits have an extra, smaller, pair of upper incisors, one on each side of the two large front ones. Rabbits also have a deep slit on their upper lip (a harelip) that shows their front teeth.*

*Because of these and other differences, scientists now place rabbits in a group called lagomorphs (from Greek words meaning "hare-shaped"), which includes rabbits, hares, and pikas. People sometimes confuse rabbits and hares, which look rather similar but are not closely related. Some are misnamed. For example, the Belgian hare is a rabbit, and the jackrabbit and snowshoe rabbit are really hares.*

43

During the Middle Ages, monks were the first to successfully domesticate rabbits. In sixteenth-century England, Queen Elizabeth I raised rabbits as pets and started a rabbit-raising fad among the nobles of her court. About 270 years ago when the selection of domestic breeds began, there were only five or six breeds. Today, there are more than fifty.

As the Europeans established colonies in other parts of the world, settlers took rabbits along with them. Soon they were thriving in North and South America, and in Australia and New Zealand as well. The rabbits that are raised all over the world as pets and food animals today are descendants of the wild European rabbits.

## A RABBIT'S LIFE

In the wild, rabbits live in grasslands and open parts of woodlands. They dig a maze of underground burrows, which crisscross and connect into a complicated community dwelling-place called a warren. Rabbits are active at night and return to their burrows in the morning to rest, groom their fur, and snuggle together in close family groups.

Rabbits, usually males, will fight to defend their home territories. The winner becomes the dominant male and makes his home with his family in the center of the warren. He then marks out his territory with special scent glands under his chin. Males are most territorial during the breeding season, from autumn to early summer. By the late summer, these males go through a change and begin to calm down and become friendly and sociable.

Rabbits live completely on plant foods. Their digestive systems are specialized to handle their vegetarian diet. Their intestines are unusually long. A special fold in the intestines, called the caecum, provides a home for bacteria that can break down cellulose. Without these helpful bacteria, rabbits could not digest plant foods, because plant cells are wrapped in a covering of tough cellulose.

## RABBITS AS PETS

Rabbits are adorable animals that are known for their long floppy ears and short bushy tail. They can vary greatly in size, from the tiny Polish rabbit weighing less than 3 pounds (1.4 kilograms) to the Flemish giant rabbit that weighs up to 17 pounds (8 kilograms). They also come in many different colors and have a variety of patterns and appearances.

By nature, rabbits are sociable animals, and they do best when they are kept in pairs. However, you've probably heard the saying "multiplying like rabbits," so if you do not want to breed rabbits, it is best to keep same sex animals. Males are likely to become aggressive when females are around. (Neutering will make males less aggressive, however.)

Rabbits are not very vocal creatures. Most of the time, you will probably not hear them make any sounds, although they may make little grunting noises if they are annoyed. They also stomp their powerful back legs on the ground if they are angry or arguing over territory.

Smaller breeds such as the Netherland dwarf, Polish, Dutch, Mini Lop, and Mini Rex breeds are probably the best choices for pet owners since they are easier to handle and take up less room. They weigh from 2 to 7 pounds (1 to 3 kilograms). Large breeds such as the Californian, the Chinchilla Giganta, the New Zealand White, and the Flemish Giant are very difficult to handle and need much more space. These animals weigh from 9 to more than 15 pounds (4 to 7 kilograms).

Rabbits that are handled frequently and taken care of properly can make great pets. Their life span is 8 to 10 years.

## INTERNET RESOURCES

http://freezone.com/kclub/purfpets/rabbits.html "Pet Rabbits"

http://members.aol.com/arbanet/arba/web/index.htm Home page of The American Rabbit Breeders Association, Inc.

http://pages.prodigy.com/NTMX83A/ "Paulson's Rabbit World"

http://www.bcyellowpages.com/advert/b/BCHES/rabbit.htm "Rabbit Care"

http://www.geocities.com/Heartland/Plains/1564/ "The Rabbit Page" (information and links)

http://www.geocities.com/Heartland/Valley/1155/Index3.html and http://www.geocities.com/Heartland/Valley/1155/Index4.html "Caring for Your Pet Rabbit" (Parts 1 and 2)

http://www.rabbit.org/ "House Rabbit Society" (information and links)

http://www.rabbitweb.net/ "The Rabbit Web" (articles, ads, chat, and links)

http://www.rabbitweb.net/patbreed.htm "What Breed Is My Bunny" by Pat Lamar

http://www.rabbitweb.net/patlamar.htm "Rabbits, Rabbits, Rabbits!" by Pat Lamar

# NOT A PET!

THE IDEA OF POCKET PETS—animals small enough to carry around with you and stow in a pocket—seems very appealing. A number of rodents and other small pets are so cute and cuddly that they look like the stuffed toys young children love. But it would be a mistake to think of these pets as a kind of plush toy come to life. They are real animals with behaviors and special needs that may not always be convenient for their owners. Indeed, some of them are not very good choices as pets for children, especially young children. A mouse or gerbil could be injured by a child playing just a bit too roughly; and a hamster or any other small rodent that gets loose in a house can quickly turn from pet into pest. Another problem to consider is the short life span of many small pet animals. Having a pet die after only a few years can bring a lot of grief.

If you decide you really would like a pocket pet, where should you get it? Ideally, the best source for any pet, especially an exotic species like a degu or duprasi or flying squirrel, is an experienced breeder who hand-raises the animals, makes sure they are healthy, and will take the time to provide all the advice you need. Breeders are not always conveniently located, though, and you may be tempted to pick up a pet at the local pet shop. Animals like mice, rats, and hamsters are quite cheap, and if something goes wrong it will not take a huge investment to get another. In fact, it is all too easy to regard them as "disposable" pets. No pet owner should have such an attitude.

It may also be tempting to bring home a small animal you find outside, especially if it seems to be in danger. You might find a litter of cottontail rabbits while cutting the grass, for example, or rescue a chipmunk your cat was playing with. Many naturalists and scientists were inspired to their careers by an experience like this. But that was before people realized how delicately balanced natural communities are, and before there were government regulations making it illegal to keep wildlife in captivity.

There are some good reasons for these laws. Well-meaning people may try to provide a good home for a squirrel or wood mouse or other wild animal but may not know the right things to do to keep it alive and healthy. And some wild animals simply can't be tamed. They do not have the right kind of temperament to live contentedly in captivity. That cute little animal you found might also hurt you. If it is frightened, it may bite you, and some animals may be carrying diseases such as rabies, or parasites such as the ticks that carry Lyme disease or Rocky Mountain spotted fever.

If you find a wild animal that seems to be lost or hurt, the best thing to do is to contact the nearest office of your state's Division of Fish, Game, and Wildlife. They will contact a licensed rehabilitator, who will be able to give the animal the care it needs. And if you're really keen on caring for wildlife, do volunteer work for a local wildlife rescue organization.

Remember that many localities do not allow certain animals to be kept, or they require pet owners to obtain special permits or licenses. You can find out the regulations for your area by calling your state wildlife agency.

# FOR FURTHER INFORMATION

*Note:* Before attempting to keep a kind of pet that is new to you, it is a good idea to read one or more pet manuals about that species. Check your local library, pet shop, or bookstore. Search for information on the species on the Internet.

## BOOKS

Burn, Barbara. *A Practical Guide to Impractical Pets.* New York: Howell Book House, 1997.

Chrystie, Frances N., and Margery Facklam. *Pets: A Comprehensive Handbook for Kids,* revised edition. Boston: Little, Brown, 1995.

Messonnier, Shawn. *Exotic Pets: A Veterinary Guide for Owners.* Plano, Texas: Wordware Publishing, 1995.

Siino, Betsy Sikora. *You Want WHAT for a Pet?!* New York: Howell Book House, 1996.

## INTERNET RESOURCES

http://dcn.davis.ca.us/vme/DrSue/pockpets.html "Dr. Sue's Pocket Pets"

http://family.disney.com/Features/family_1997_10/Inkd/Inkd107pets/Inkd107 pets.html Charleen Engberg, "Lincoln Kids—Pocket Pets"

http://www.nwlink.com/~pawprint/petparts_b4ubuy.html "Before You Buy" (things to consider before getting a pet)

http://www.rmca.org/Resources/abestpet.txt Angela Horn, "Which Pet Rodent?"

http://www.webcom.com/lstead/rodents/general.html "Caring for a Rodent"

http://www.webcom.com/lstead/rodents/roundup.html "Rodent Roundup: A Comparative Guide to Critters"

# INDEX

Page numbers in *italics* refer to illustrations.

African dormouse, 33
African pygmy mouse, 32–33
agouti, 40
Aharoni, Israel, 15, 16

Belgian hare, 43
brown rat (*see* rat)
brush-tail rat (*see* degu)

caecum, 44
Californian rabbit, 45
Campbell's hamster, 17
captive breeding, 8
cavies (*see* guinea pig)
Chapman, Mathias F., 8
chinchilla, *6*, 6–9
Chinchilla Giganta rabbit, 45
Chinese hamster, 17
clawed jird, 20
cottontail rabbit, 44

degu, *10*, 10–13, 46
diabetes, 12
dormouse, 33
duprasi, *22*, 22–25, 46
Dutch rabbit, 45
dwarf Russian hamster, 17

endangered species, 8

fancy mice, 32
fat-tailed gerbil (*see* duprasi)
Flemish giant rabbit, 44–45
flying squirrel, *34*, 34–37, 46

gerbil, *18*, 18–21, 46
giant African pouched rat, 29

guinea pig, *38*, 38–41

hamster, *14*, 14–17, 46
hare, 43, 44

jackrabbit, 43, 44

laboratory animals, 27, 39
lagomorphs, 43
lizard, 11

Mini Lop rabbit, 45
Mini Rex rabbit, 45
Mongolian gerbil (*see* gerbil)
mouse, *30*, 30–33, 46

Netherland dwarf rabbit, 45
New Zealand White rabbit, 45
northern flying squirrel (*see* flying squirrel)
Norway rat (*see* rat)

Octodontidae, 11

Polish rabbit, 44, 45

rabbit, *42*, 42–45
rat, *26*, 26–29, 46
rock rat (*see* degu)
rodents, 7

Schwentker, Victor, 19
snowshoe rabbit, 43
southern flying squirrel (*see* flying squirrel)
Syrian hamster (*see* hamster)

teeth, 7, 43
Tumblebrook Farm, 19

wild animals, 46–47